Bernstein and poetics revisited

Jan Blommaert

First published in 2007 by the Institute of Education, University of London,
20 Bedford Way, London WC1H 0AL
www.ioe.ac.uk/publications

© Institute of Education, University of London 2007

British Library Cataloguing in Publication Data:
A catalogue record for this publication is available from the British Library

ISBN 978 0 85473 791 8

Jan Blommaert asserts the moral right to be identified as the author of this work.

Typeset by Keystroke, 28 High Street, Tettenhall, Wolverhampton

Printed by Elanders Ltd.

Institute of Education • University of London

Bernstein and poetics revisited

Voice, globalisation and education

Jan Blommaert

Professor of Languages in Education

Based on a Professorial Lecture delivered at the Institute of Education,
University of London on 6 November 2007

Professor Jan Blommaert

Introduction

In a remarkably careful and delicate essay entitled 'Bernstein and poetics', Dell Hymes (1996: Chapter 9) discussed the merits of Basil Bernstein's work. According to Hymes (as we know, the founding father of sociolinguistic ethnography and an innovator in the field of language in education), Bernstein ought to be credited for something often overlooked in critical readings of his work: the attention he gave to language as a concrete resource which is differentially distributed as to access and command, and to the ways in which differences in *how* people talked often led to differences in the value attributed to their talk. Bernstein, according to Hymes, had shown that language in its 'crude' shape – language with an accent, a particular lexis, a set of grammatical peculiarities – was not only an object of difference, but one of inequality as well. Consequently, the concrete modes of appearance of language ought to be central to our concerns in the field of language in education, and Hymes laments (like Bernstein before him) the rather baffling absence of scholarly attention to the issue of variation-as-inequality in and through language:

> The transformation of society to a juster, more equal way of life requires transformation of genuine inequalities in verbal resource. But – here is the crux – we know very little about the actual distribution of verbal resource and ability in our society. We know too little to be able

to specify the complex ways in which such a distribution becomes a source of inequality.

(Hymes 1996: 46–7)

We have come some way since Hymes voiced his complaints. Work such as that of Hymes himself, James Gee, James Collins, Shirley Brice Heath and Ben Rampton (to name just a few) has laid the foundations for a critical study of real language in real educational circumstances. We have now come closer to an understanding of the nuts and bolts of linguistic variation as a factor in assessment, appraisal and evaluation in education, and we have started to understand that there are complex and often unpredictable connections between modes of occurrence of language, and evaluative qualifications such as 'under-achiever' or 'intelligent learner'. We have started to understand the ways in which concrete language forms give rise to inhabited and ascribed identities, and how some forms of language enable some identities and disable others.

Yet, Hymes' lament can be repeated today, perhaps even with an even greater sense of urgency. The object we call 'language' is still understood by many as a uniform, closed, bounded and rule-governed phenomenon – a single dot on a line, or a closed box – and unfortunately the many also include policy makers, here as well as elsewhere. This is remarkable, because great metropolitan urban centres all over the world (London is of course one of them) are increasingly becoming the homes of almost any imaginable form of linguistic variation, due to what we now call globalisation. We witness an increasing diversification in populations – 'super-diversity' (Vertovec 2006) – and with it an increasing diversification in language choices, forms of communicative behaviour, new varieties of vernacular languages such as English, and new forms of locality and translocality that create new speech communities and networks. Add to this the increasing diversification of literacy due to the massification of electronic and otherwise multimodal channels of communication, and one understands that almost any existing linguistic and sociolinguistic insight is fundamentally challenged by globalisation. And in the face of such growing conceptual and empirical instability, remarkably, we see how more and more authorities (including academic ones, I add with regret) withdraw to the safe fortresses of homogeneism: one culture-one language models, in which language is a stable, bounded, singular item, and in which 'knowing' the language becomes a self-evident condition for any sort of qualification of normalcy. Unless you speak our language (well), you won't be a citizen, a good student, a member of my neighbourhood, a human being worthy of consideration.[1]

Here is the problem: a fundamentally new environment is being described by means of concepts and models that weren't even adequate to address the old environment (recall that Bernstein addressed intra-community class differences). As always, education becomes a battlefield where such tensions are being played out, unfortunately in a battle that seems to count only losers. And as scholars of language in education, we are facing the challenge to get our act together and to redefine our toolkit. It won't perhaps win the battle, but someone has to prepare for peace.

Voice, not choice

Let us first establish one main point. In considering language in society, the emphasis must be on *function*, that is: on what real people really do with real bits and pieces of linguistic and semiotic material. This is only seemingly unproblematic and self-evident. As soon as we turn to the traditions of scholarship on language, the issue becomes quite thorny, for linguistics has been notably taciturn on issues of linguistic functions (exceptions such as Halliday and Dik prove the rule). Hymes (1996: 45) comments: 'many linguists proceed as if mankind became more unified each time they used the word *universal*, freer and more capable of solving its problems each time they invoked linguistic competence and creativity'.

It is too easy to state that 'language serves as an instrument for producing meanings'. The essential question is: which particular meanings? And how exactly does language serve that purpose? How do people actually use language to produce meanings? And how come they do that in so many different ways? What, in short, has language in actual practice to offer to real humans? 'Meaning' in itself is a very weak and uninformative answer to that.

A concept such as 'voice' may offer us more value for money. People use language and other semiotic means in attempts to have voice, to make themselves understood by others. This process is complex and only partly predictable, because whatever is produced is not necessarily perceived or understood, and having voice is therefore an intrinsically social process – that is a process with clear connections to social structure, history, culture, power. This is of course Bakhtin's dialogic practice, and while many 'Bakhtin-light' interpretations exist, I suggest a high-calorie, Bourdieuan, interpretation. Voice is a social product, and it is therefore not unified but subject to processes of selection and exclusion that have their feet firmly in social structure. Consequently, voice is best seen materialistically as the practical conversion of socially 'loaded' resources into socially 'loaded' semiotic action, every aspect of which shows traces of the patterns of distribution of the resources. Some resources will be exclusive, others will be democratic; some will mark superiority, others inferiority; some will function well across different social contexts while others' functions are locked into specific niches in society. Some people will have a lot, others will have few; some have valuable resources while others have low-value resources. The dialogue to which Bakhtin referred is thus not just a meeting of different voices on neutral ground: it is a social and political diagnostic that is played out in a field which is never neutral but always someone's home turf. The rules of the dialogue are rarely democratically established; they are more often imposed, either by force or by consensus. It is at this latter point that history, culture and ideology enter the picture: every social context is normative, and most contexts are normative because the norms are seen as 'normal' (see Blommaert (2005) for an extensive discussion). Thus whenever we open our mouths, we not only use and re-use the words of others, but we also place ourselves firmly in a recognisable social context from which and to which all kinds of messages flow – indexical aspects of meaning, conventional (i.e. social, cultural, historical etc.) links established between communication and the social context in which it takes place.

Voice as a concept offers us a 'praxis' metaphor of meaning: meaning as invested with real interests and as 'theoretically' mediated, that is, as organised on the basis of ideological patterns of normativity. Communication, thus, is

4

what people make of it, and people do that under all kinds of real-world constraints. It is clear that an illiterate person has a different potential for voice from a literate person; that a multilingual person has different potential from a monolingual one; that someone who speaks the prestige variety of a language has a different potential from someone who speaks a stigmatised and marginalised variety of the language, and so forth. Institutions have the tendency to 'freeze' the conditions for voice: unless you speak or write *in this particular way*, you won't be heard or read. Imposed normativity is a feature of most institutions, and the education system is generally a case in point (which prompted Bourdieu and Passeron (1977) to see it as a system of ideological reproduction).

Imposed normativity, to be sure, is rarely a monolith, and even more rarely does it survive time. Regimes do change – politically, economically but also linguistically and sociolinguistically. Thus, while the moment-to-moment deployment of normative complexes only suggests stability (each suspect is interviewed by the police in very similar ways), the medium-to-long run can and does show dramatic shifts. In the context of globalisation, such shifts should be kept in focus: we must analyse where they occur and where they do not occur, and why they are successful or failures whenever they occur.

Let us first turn to two examples of institutional language regimes and what effects they have on voice. We have to do this in order to grasp the basic mechanisms at play here: the dynamics of voice, constraints and affordances in relation to social, cultural, historical conditions.

Vulnerable voices

Losing voice: immigrants and the police

As said above, institutions usually impose constraints on what and how people can communicate in relation to them. The more 'central' institutions are in a society, the stronger one can expect such normative imposition to be. Courts, parliaments, police and security services (but also banks, insurance companies, major industries) operate by means of a streamlined and uniformised set of communicative routines. Often, precisely this uniformity in communication practices is used to claim self-qualifications of being democratic and equitable: the same rule is applied to 'everyone', and the suggestion is that when this is guaranteed, no one will be excluded.

There is, however, no single set of linguistic resources that is totally democratic. Even very basic resources such as fluency in the local language are differentially distributed, with some people being real experts and most people being rather mediocre talkers (which explains why we differentiate constantly between such categories in our own social environment); more advanced resources such as literacy skills are even more severely affected by various forms of inequality. And while bureaucracies claim to develop their language regimes on grounds of reasonable assumptions about average proficiency and skills levels among their target populations, too often such average levels are, in actual practice, those of an educated middle class. Those who have had to deal with bureaucracies in 'difficult cases' know what I am talking about: the mountain of paper, the multiple procedural steps and the necessary recourse to bodies of intertextual information (rules, procedures, jurisprudence, expertise, laws) all put tremendous pressure on the actual language and literacy resources one controls. Bureaucratic language regimes are mostly very demanding ones, and they thus often exclude those who needed access most.

Globalisation exposes this by offering us spectacular examples of widespread structural problems. Immigrants from various parts of the world enter in a bureaucratic space where their own linguistic and sociolinguistic resources may deviate strongly from the presupposed ones. Usually, this deviation is negative: they do *not* have the required resources to accomplish the complex tasks in front of them. Consider the following example, a handwritten police declaration by a 35-year-old woman from Congo.[2]

The woman had been arrested on grounds of shoplifting. In the Belgian legal system, everyone has the right to go on record with his/her own account. That means: one would be asked whether one 'can write', and if so, one would be invited to write one's own account of the events. This document, then, becomes a legally consequential element in the criminal prosecution case: it is 'the story of the accused' and both the defence lawyer and the prosecution will refer to it as such. Observe that under Belgian law, suspects have the right to write in a language of their choice. In this case, the woman obviously confirmed that she 'could write', and she chose to write in Lingala, the lingua franca of Kinshasa and of the Congolese diaspora.

The phrase 'can write', however, is deceptively simple. In a country such as Congo, literacy skills are generally rare and access to advanced and sophisticated forms of literacy is severely restricted. That means: while Congolese say they 'can write' when they are able to perform basic writing skills, that description would not cover the production of a long, nuanced and detailed written narrative in a standard, normative language variety and a standard orthography. Let us have a closer look at what and how the woman wrote. Here is a transcript of the text, followed by a translation. In the transcript I will try to preserve the graphic features of the original:

BaKANGI NGAI NAYIBI, eZALI YALOKUTA
baKANGI NGAI na bilamba minei
4 Pantalon na yebi [nb]atu te moSuSu
oyo baZALAKI na MAGASIN te

They caught me (because) I had stolen, that is a lie
They caught me with four pieces of clothing
4 *pantalons* I don't know the other people
who were with me in the *magasin*

The woman – even if her writing was procedurally prefaced by a clear affirmation that she 'could write' – obviously struggles with several very basic literacy requirements. There is orthographic instability articulated through the alteration of uppercase and lowercase; punctuation is erratic, and several corrections betray a struggle with the grammatical and narrative norms she knows are at play here. She also switches to French – 'pantalons', 'magasin' – and so offers us a glimpse of the vernacular everyday (but 'non-standard') Lingala she speaks. And finally, she manifestly fails to produce a narrative that can stand as her 'account of the events'. There is no sequential development of actions, no plot nor storyline, no argued conclusion. The woman has written *something*, but in the legal procedure this something will not be of much use to her. Her writing has failed to produce voice, and writing here silences her voice.[3] The simple question 'can you write?' seems to be one that does not withstand the test of globalisation. Answers to it refer to practices and skills that belong to local, and very divergent, economies of literacy. Institutional regimes that emphasise uniformity in communication practices will exclude, marginalise and silence people whose repertoires do not match the normative expectations. Globalisation is likely to intensify this form of exclusion, because the super-diversity it spawns precludes any presupposability of linguistic or literacy resources among growing numbers of people.

Getting voice: witnesses in the TRC proceedings

Regimes can change, however, and – though such occasions are rare – previously silenced voices may be given space and recognition. The transition from Apartheid to a democratic predisposition in South Africa produced such a shift in conditions for voice. Previously silenced people could speak out, and their words were respected as important and formative for the new society – the post-Apartheid society saw the celebration of ordinary people as architects of peace, freedom and tolerance. Closer inspection of such events and their conditions, however, yield a rather more nuanced picture. Let us consider a fragment from a testimony given by a lady during a televised hearing of the South-African Truth and Reconciliation Commission (TRC). The TRC was seen as (and both celebrated and criticised because of) an opportunity for formerly oppressed people to speak. This was specifically the case in the Human Rights Violations hearings, in which victims of Apartheid brutalities – members of opposition organisations as well as ordinary people – were offered a public forum. Chaired by prestige figures such as Desmond Tutu and Alex Boraine, such ordinary people were given respect, occasion and time to produce voice.

The particular piece of data I shall discuss here is taken from the official transcript of the hearing, archived on the website of the TRC (Truth and Reconciliation Commission, UWC Hearing – Day 1 – Monday 5 August 1996. Case Nr. CT/00222). The lady in question is Maureen Cupido, the mother of a boy who got accidentally shot during riots in the Cape Town area in August 1985. Maureen Cupido was a 'coloured' woman living in the townships in the Cape area.[4] What follows is the 'core' story produced by Maureen Cupido – her account of the events of August 1985. This fragment was preceded by a number of introductory questions and followed by some questions for clarification from the TRC panel, to which we shall return later. I have adopted the version from the official transcript, but in view of the discussion below I have inserted numbers indicating narrative episodes, and I have underscored a number of utterances.

(1) Well I was sitting, and me and my husband <u>was sitting</u> waiting for Clive to come home. Because that's the day <u>that</u> Boesak and Tutu had the march in Cape Town. (2) Clive came home early – <u>eleven o'clock the morning</u> and then he told me this march is going to have a lot of trouble. <u>Little knowing</u> that he is going to be killed (3) and then he went to this friend and he sat – he first then have supper and then he went to his friend, and that was early hours, early. (4) And then we – we wait for Clive to come home, because my husband never sits, wait for his children, I am the only one. (5) And then suddenly I just fell asleep and then I stood up and I went to my bedroom and as I went to my bedroom to get onto my bed, I heard the shots, because before the shots, (my heart) gave three – three thumps, I just – my heart just went you know. (6) And then I asked God if it's my child, take him away, I don't want him to be paralyzed. <u>Little knowing</u> it was my child. (7) And just after the shots, <u>this chaps, this children running</u> to our house and all they said, Ms Cupido is Clive here. I told them no. (8) But they didn't want to say anything, they just asked and I – I couldn't go, it was

say past eleven (9) and then my husband and my daughter, they took the car and they went out with the car to the hospital. Because apparently they didn't come tell us our son was shot, no-one came to tell us. They came to fetch the body already, but now my husband went straight to the hospital, Tygerberg. (10) Apparently when he came there, he and my daughter – so when they saw him, so he asked one of the porters if here – a body came in here, they didn't want to answer him. But he said he could of smelled the death, he could of smelled the death when he passed that certain ambulance. (11) And then they pushed the ambulance through the door and then the nurses came out and they all barricaded the ambulance so that this people in the car couldn't see which – who is in the ambulance. (12) But my husband recognized my son's hair, because he's got – he had lovely black hair, he just saw the hair. (13) And apparently when he went inside, this Lawrence Davids was sitting there, he was so shocked to see my husband and he asked what happened. And my husband didn't answer him. (14) And it's only afterwards when the body went into the hospital that they said, the next morning they said he was dead. (15) So we had to go to Salt River Mortuary to identify my husband – my son's body. (16) That's all.

Mrs Cupido's narrative is what some would call a 'subaltern' narrative, produced by someone who appears to be far from an 'ideal' speaker. The transcript was verbatim, and it contains traces of spoken working-class varieties of South African English, underscored in the fragment above. The transcriber, for instance, writes 'this' in 'this chaps, this children' and 'this people in the car', where probably a phonetic realization of /diːs/ ('these') would have been heard on tape. Similarly, the transcriber wrote 'of' in 'he could of smelled the death', where a colloquial realization of 'have' as /ʼaf/ would be heard on tape. Mrs Cupido also produces grammatically non-standard expressions such as 'me and my husband was sitting' as well as a number of awkward constructions and expressions, such as 'eleven o'clock the morning', 'that certain ambulance', 'they pushed the ambulance through the door' and 'they all barricaded the ambulance'. The phrase 'this people in the car' is referentially opaque and the function of the demonstrative in 'this Lawrence Davids' is also unclear. Finally, Mrs Cupido uses two stock expressions that seem to be borrowed from another, more formal, Standard English register: 'Little knowing' and 'apparently' in utterances such as 'And apparently when he went inside, this Lawrence Davids was sitting there'. This phenomenon of 'cross-register transfer' (a form of Bourdieu's 'hypercorrection') has been noted in other African English sources as well and it indexes lower social class as well as non-native competence (two things that often go hand in hand) (Bourdieu 1991; Blommaert 1998).

Mrs Cupido has limited linguistic-communicative resources in the code expected in a televised interview. She also has limited resources when it comes to another aspect of the TRC hearings: the production of political statements. Mrs Cupido produces no grand political message about the reform of the South African society. One of the routine ingredients of the public hearings was a question on what the TRC could do for the victims. Whereas some victims used that slot for formulating explicit political statements, Mrs Cupido answers the question from a personal and local perspective:

> Commissioner Burton: What is it that you would like the Truth Commission to do?
>
> Maureen Cupido: As you know Clive wasn't – I haven't got such brilliant children, but his whole aim was that he, he wanted to go and work, he was frustrated, he wanted to make his ten finished and then he told me, mommy you can't afford to sent me to a varsity, but I'll go and work and I'll do part-time, I'll do part-time varsity, so I am going to work to help you, you see. That was his aim, he just wanted to finish up his standard ten. And I mean I – I feel that the truth must come out, people should know that it wasn't my son that kept the policeman, it was Lawrence Davids, but seeing that it was a State of Emergency that's why his parents didn't want him to come and testify, so the truth must come out, it must come out, he must be – they must see to him and he must give a statement and – and Errol van Rensburg.

Of course, this statement reveals lots of political meanings. It shows, for instance, the extent of the hegemony of the Apartheid state, when something that was later framed as a human rights violation could be perceived and experienced for years as a family and neighbourhood problem. It also indicates a shift in the conditions for voice. The TRC was explicitly aimed at constructing voice. People who had no voice previously could now address the nation and make politically consequential statements; versions of history that were forbidden or remained unsaid now received a forum for public (and legitimate) expression. The shift in conditions on sayability is explicitly oriented to by Mrs Cupido. At one point in the interview she tells how, years ago, she knew and told the facts of the incident. Then this sequence follows:

> Chair: Now do you know of anybody who specifically heard that?
> Maureen Cupido: We know and we approached the people but the – the day of the Court case they didn't want to come forward. I can't blame the people because that time it was State of Emergency and I mean everybody was frightened to go to jail.

Mrs Cupido's story was unsayable under Apartheid: Mrs Cupido was coloured and her son was killed during political riots – events on which the regime was notoriously monological. Furthermore she could not speak out, being a working-class woman with no means of getting access to the media or to international public opinion channels. Mrs Cupido was probably completely unknown prior to the TRC hearing.

The poetics of voice
So how exactly does Maureen Cupido speak out? If we take a look at the overall narrative architecture, we notice a clear and transparent development of the sequence of events. Here is a critical move: we already observed the 'subaltern' linguistic and political characteristics of Maureen Cupido's story. She speaks from within a working-class, marginalised minority world, as a deeply hurt victim of oppression and violence. A full understanding of the voice she articulates, however, must take into account the full range of resources that Mrs

Cupido displays and deploys. In other words: we need to extend the scope and range of what we consider to be competence, including, here, *narrative* competence. What follows is an 'ethnopoetic' transcript of Mrs Cupido's story – a transcript in which formal markers of her speech are seen as structural elements of a narrative, divided into episodes, verses, stanzas and lines (see Hymes (1996, 2003) and Blommaert (2005)).

Well I was sitting,   1
and me and my husband was sitting
   waiting for Clive to come home.
      Because that's the day that Boesak and Tutu had the march
      in Cape Town.

Clive came home early –   2
   eleven o'clock the morning
and then he told me
   this march is going to have a lot of trouble.
      Little knowing that he is going to be killed

and then he went to this friend   3
and he sat –
   he first then have supper
and then he went to his friend,
   and that was early hours, early.

And then we – we wait for Clive to come home,   4
   because my husband never sits, wait for his children,
   I am the only one.

And then suddenly I just fell asleep   5
and then I stood up
and I went to my bedroom
and as I went to my bedroom to get onto my bed,

I heard the shots,
  because before the shots,
  (my heart) gave three – three thumps,
  I just – my heart just went you know.

And <u>then</u> I asked God   6
  if it's my child, take him away,
  I don't want him to be paralyzed.
    Little knowing it was my child.

And just after the shots,   7
this chaps, this children running to our house
and all they said,
  Ms Cupido is Clive here.
I told them no.

But they didn't want to say anything,   8
they just asked
and I – I couldn't go,
  it was say past eleven

<u>**and**</u> <u>then</u> my husband and my daughter, they took the car   9
and they went out with the car to the hospital.
  Because apparently they didn't come tell us our son was shot,
  no-one came to tell us.
They came to fetch the body already,
but now my husband went straight to the hospital, Tygerberg.

Apparently when he came there,   10
  he and my daughter
so when they saw him,
so he asked one of the porters
  if here – a body came in here,

they didn't want to answer him.
But he said
    he could of smelled the death,
    he could of smelled the death
        when he passed that certain ambulance.

And <u>then</u> they pushed the ambulance through the door   11
<u>**and**</u> <u>then</u> the nurses came out
and they all barricaded the ambulance
    so that this people in the car couldn't see
        which – who is in the ambulance.

But my husband recognized my son's hair,   12
    because he's got – he had lovely black hair,
he just saw the hair.

And apparently when he went inside,   13
this Lawrence Davids was sitting there,
    he was so shocked to see my husband
and he asked what happened.
And my husband didn't answer him.

And it's only afterwards   14
    when the body went into the hospital
that they said,
the next morning they said
    he was dead.

So we had to go to Salt River Mortuary to identify my husband –
my son's body,   15

that's all.   16

Mrs Cupido starts with sketching a setting (unit 1), and then develops a clear and well-structured account of the unfolding of events. All the units in the narrative are factual, with the exception of unit 6 ('and then I asked God') and the concluding metapragmatic statement 'that's all' (unit 16). But the structuring is done with minimal resources: most of the marking of narrative units, events and moves in the narrative is done by means of the connective discourse marker 'and' or 'and then'. The whole build-up of the narrative is simple and terse. Only one metaphorical emotive expression is used: '(my heart) gave three – three thumps, I just – <u>my heart just went</u> you know', and once an emotive state is expressed in the shape of a prayer (unit 6). Each of the units ('stanzas' in ethnopoetic terminology) contains a coherent step in the unfolding of the narrative. The intensive use of 'and (then)' punctuates a rhythm to the story: Mrs Cupido tries to be precise and factual by providing declarative statements sequentially ordered in time ('and (then)').

Let us look more closely at some parts of the story. The stanzas 8, 10, 12 and 15 deviate from the general structure of the story in which, as we saw, the marker 'and (then)' provides the main coherence element. Let us take a closer look at stanza 10; I will mark some formal features with bold and with arrows, and will divide the fragment in three different parts:

(1)
Apparently when he came there,
    he and my daughter
(2)
so when they saw him,
so he asked one of the porters
    if here – a body came in here,
they didn't want to answer him.
(3)
But he said
    he could of smelled the death,   ⇐
    he could of smelled the death   ⇐
        when he passed that certain ambulance.

We note three features:

(i) The fragment has a clear episodic structure, sequential in time. Part (1) precedes parts (2) and (3). It is in itself a micro-narrative.

(ii) This is further supported by two narrative devices: (a) a contrast in leading discourse marker ('apparently') between stanza 10 and its preceding and following stanzas, which both follow the general dominance of 'and' as a leading marker. The episode in stanza 10 is clearly marked as separate by Mrs Cupido; (b) the internal alteration of markers which divides stanza 10 into three parts: 'apparently' – 'so' – 'but'.

(iii) It also culminates in the repeated line of indirect speech 'he could of smelled the death' (marked by arrows).

Let us stop to examine the third feature. This repetition is a micro-shift in performance style. This is 'pure' repetition: a repetition that marks emphasis; compare it to other instances of repetition in Mrs Cupido's narrative – in stanzas 3 and 14 – where each of the repetitions is aimed at adding detail to the statement. Compare it now to stanza 12:

> But my husband recognized my son's **hair**,
> because he's got – he had lovely black **hair**,
> he just saw the **hair**.

Again we see repetition here, a mixed form in which the second line adds detail to the first while the third line is a 'pure' repetition of the motif set in the first. Again it is a breakthrough into a different kind of performance (Hymes 1981: Chapter 3), a microscopic one, but significant. It is at these moments of minimal shifting that we hear a different voice: that of a mother severely injured by a decade of suffering over the tragic loss of her son. It was the voice we also heard in the second half of stanza 5 (her heart pounding) and in stanza 6 where she reports her prayer when she heard the shots.

Maureen Cupido, like the Congolese woman in the previous section, produces her story under crushing constraints. She is a working-class woman who for years felt the pressure of her community while she had to cope with the loss of her son; now she is staged in a mass-mediated event of national significance, and she has to speak in front of TV cameras, a large audience, and a panel of distinguished TRC commissioners. She produces her statements in a monotonous, reporting delivery style and she does not shed a tear. Her narrative is an attempt at producing a factual, evidential account of the events, and that explains the repetitions in which she adds detail to her statements. She only breaks out of this factual and evidential frame in the stanzas 6, 8 and 10, and does so by minimal stylistic shifts: by quoting her prayer and by means of shifts in the leading discourse markers and in the patterns of repetition. Such minimal shifts were described by Goffman as shifts in 'footing' (Goffman 1981); we can also describe them as shifts in voice through micro-shifts in genre, from factual reporting to a more emotional narrative genre.

Let us now try to perform a similar analysis on the Congolese woman's statement. Her statement, like Mrs Cupido's, is a narrative, and this becomes clear when we transpose it in ethnopoetic representation:

BaKANGI NGAI
NAYIBI
eZALI YALOKUTA

baKANGI NGAI na bilamba minei
4 Pantalon

na yebi [nb]atu te moSuSu oyo baZALAKI na MAGASIN te

In translation, the story would sound as follows:

They caught me
(because) I had stolen
that is a lie

They caught me with four pieces of clothing
4 *pantalons*

I don't know the other people who were with me in the *magasin*

The woman produces two narrative motifs: (i) the fact that she got caught; and (ii) the fact that she doesn't know the other people in the shop. While the second motif is developed in one line only, the first motif is elaborated. It is spread over two 'verses'; the first verse expresses a judgement ('that is a lie'), the second one clarifies the factual side of it ('with four pieces of clothing – 4 pantalons').

In all likelihood, the two motifs mirror the elements of the accusation against her: that she stole four pieces of clothing, and that she did so in connivance with other people. These elements are both stated and commented upon: she refutes both claims, while she reproduces the claims. The text, thus, narrates the events in a direct dialogue with the police, and so provides a *response* to accusations rather than just a factual account of the events. Generically, this is a misfit: the refutation of the accusations needs to be done by a lawyer in court, *on the basis of* the written statement of the defendant. The Congolese woman defends herself, she uses a voice that isn't hers to use, and consequently silences herself. But of course we hear her, as well as the police, in this micro-story: we hear the voice of the accuser and the voice of the defendant blended in a generically dislodged text. The blending is expressed in the use of the third person plural inflections – '*they* caught me' – in a direct dialogue with those who caught her ('*you* caught me'). The 'they' creates a narrative frame, while the denials create a responsive and moral frame. And so the 'I' in the text is both a character in a story ('they caught *me*') and a moral, evaluating subject who qualifies the police's claims as 'a lie'. Even if the text is extremely short and seems to contain hardly any 'information', we see different voices at work in it, and the grammatical and textual slippage from 'them' to 'you' is also an instance of change of footing.

The different voices again can only be distinguished on the basis of details. When making sense, people produce lots of such details, and the details rather than the 'big' things seem to matter most. We can hear Maureen Cupido as a mother only when we attend to hardly noticeable details and the same applies when we want to understand the Congolese woman as a moral subject. The point is: what are mere details for the analyst can be crucial features for the communicator. People make sense by means of every resource they have at their disposal. The range of such resources can differ greatly, but similar procedures apply: use all there is to be used (Hymes 2003). Voice is articulated through a repertoire – big or small, simple or sophisticated. And the nature and structure of such repertoires is something that needs to be established empirically; it can never be taken for granted.

The fact is, however, that this basic truth is often overlooked in analysis, and that advanced analytical technique is required to bring about the minutiae of such voice-work. The technique I have used here is an ethnographic technique, a technique that establishes voice 'from below', so to speak, and that thus avoids quick generalisations about genre, function and form. More common approaches, for instance those that guide the training of police people and asylum application interviewers, would stress the transparency of genres – the interview, the witness statement, the written declaration under oath – and would then quickly dismiss the response as a matter of choice: 'you *chose* to answer in this way'.[5] That there is too much presumed universalism and a wealth of facile and unsubstantiated claims about the transparency of communication in these approaches is too evident to warrant much discussion. In the present world, however, we seem to be confronted more and more with instances of such communicative silliness – with devastating effects on subjects who face them.

Globalisation and making sense in classrooms

The nature and structure of repertoires cannot be taken for granted; they need to be established empirically, that is, ethnographically. As I said before, this point becomes awfully clear when we consider globalisation phenomena. The written text by the Congolese woman was a typical globalisation product: a text produced by someone from Congo, in Belgium on official police stationery. There is migration history in this small document, as well as the brutal realities of bureaucracy that surround these migrations in an age of super-diversity. And we see how a woman from Congo deploys 'Congolese' literacy skills in a Belgian institutional context, with predictable results: while such literacy performances may be adequate in Congo, they are not so in Belgium. Thus, the text shows us two other features of globalisation:

(i)   the fact that existing inequalities in the world system extend from mate-
      rial to symbolic domains when people become mobile in globalisation
      processes; and
(ii) the fact that we can no longer make any a priori assumptions about the
      repertoires of people in globalisation contexts.

As for the first element: the issue of mobility in globalisation is not just one of
capital, goods and services, but also one of language and other cultural resources
for meaning-making. An expanding literature spearheaded by Appadurai (1996)
and Castells (1997) examines such cultural forms in globalisation (but very often
bypasses the fact that, generally speaking, these cultural resources don't seem to
travel well). As for (ii) above: this means that what within a choice paradigm
would be difference needs to be seen as inequality. When people do not make
sense, it is often not because they don't *want* to make sense (or *choose* to state
things their way) but because they don't have access to the means required for
making sense *here*, in this actual context with these actual interlocutors.

   Schools, naturally, are such an actual context with actual interlocutors, and
the problems of symbolic mobility we detected earlier can be expected there
too. And given the highly regimented nature of what goes on in schools, we can
expect quite a few problems in an environment in which the presupposability of
the pupils' resources decreases. Regimentation means that more and more
things need to be made presupposable, linear and stable – while the conditions
for achieving such stability seem not to be satisfied. The bottom line about
schools and education systems all around the world is still uniformising parts
of the population within a nation-state organisational framework and with
increasing diversity in the school population; this bottom line may be more and
more a privilege of those who are already mainstream. Note that this attempt
towards uniformisation ('mainstreaming') is seen as *democratic*: when an
education system has achieved total absorption of its population into the mainstream, it is judged to have contributed to democracy. The attempt is thus
evidently not just pedagogical, but also political.[6]

   I will examine two examples that demonstrate the complexities of the issues
involved here, and the examples instantiate the two directions of globalisation:

from the centre to the periphery, and from the periphery to the centre. From the centre to the periphery we see flows of symbols, systems and instruments that are supposed to be the essence of globalisation: presumed universal recipes for development, democracy, success, leadership – things that Appadurai called 'ideoscapes' (1996). From the periphery to the centre we see migration flows, people from all over the world entering the prosperous and exclusive territories of 'the West', bringing along their material and cultural resources – language.

Mainstreaming a township school

I will turn to some data from South Africa now, where for the past few years teams of students under my supervision have done school-based fieldwork in the townships surrounding Cape Town (the same habitat, incidentally, as that of Mrs Cupido).[7] The advantage of using data from South Africa is that they offer us a magnified image of more general processes. The pedagogical and political ramifications of mainstreaming in education are plainly understood by educational researchers around the world; in some places, however, these processes and phenomena appear in a more outspoken and radical form – South Africa is a case in point. In South Africa, educational reform was one of the key elements in the transition from Apartheid to a more democratic disposition. Given its history of mass marginalisation of the non-white population, equality in education trajectories was perceived as an absolute must for building a more just and equitable society. The method chosen by the post-Apartheid governments sounds familiar: mainstreaming. All schools would be required to offer one national curriculum, and Outcome Based Education (OBE) was introduced to ensure that the actual practice of teaching and learning was both sufficiently uniform and flexible to cater for all learners.[8] The target of this post-Apartheid education system is a level of education that fits a middle-class profile – 'mainstreaming' here as almost everywhere else means absorption into the middle class. And not surprisingly, English is often seen as the key to gaining access to the mainstream: there is colossal awe for and belief in the upwardly mobile power of English (see Blommaert *et al.* (2005)).

The point I wish to establish in what follows is this: globalised resources such as English and literacy skills enter particular environments and get transformed there – 'glocalised', to use a well-established but not necessarily appropriate term. What happens is the absorption of such resources into an economy of symbolic resources that conditions these resources. Concretely: literacy resources may enter a symbolic economy in which *illiteracy* is the default situation, acquiring function and value in relation to that economy. The functions and values of literacy in a largely illiterate symbolic economy are likely to be different from those in a fully saturated literacy environment, and the same resources – 'literacy skills' – may consequently be *fundamentally different as ingredients of a repertoire* across different segments of the population. The idea of mainstreaming – disseminating 'the same' resources across the whole of the population – is then an illusion.

Let us take a look at some examples, taken from a small corpus of 53 short essays written by 12-year-old primary school pupils from a Cape Town township and collected by my student Lin Goethals in 2006. The topic is 'what I want to be when I'm big'. The township in which this research was done is a new social housing settlement started in 1999 in an attempt to 'de-slumify' the Cape Town area. The township houses newly immigrated people from the whole of the region, and in terms of the old (but persisting) colour categorisation the population would be 'coloured' and 'black'. The everyday vernacular language in this settlement would be a local variety of Afrikaans, but this occurs in a densely multilingual context where dozens of other languages are being used. For most if not all pupils who chose to take the English-medium classes (as opposed to the Afrikaans-medium ones – the education system is mandatory multilingual), English is a foreign language.

The 53 samples display enormous differences in what we can call 'fluency' in English writing. Consider examples 1–4.

We see, in this uniform school population, pupils such as those in 1 and 2 who clearly master the conventions of writing: they write sentences in a stable orthography, using some of the conventions of writing such as punctuation and the use of capitals in the first word of a sentence. But we also see pupils such as in 3, where the writing is restricted to pidginized forms and in 4, where we are facing near-illiteracy. The use of uniform age-grades in the newly democratic school system obviously hides severe and fundamental differences between the pupils.

I want to be a teacher.
I wanted to hit the children who are rude in my class.
I will never be a bad teacher to the children in my class. I want a neat class.
I want no bad smells in my class.
I want the children to wash every day.
I want to be a good teacher

Example 1

I want to be a teacher so that I can teach the chidren like my teacher teach me. And I want to teach them what my teacher teach me And I would like to teach childre that will listen to me every day.

Example 2

1. I soccer
2. I police
3. I box
4. I player
5. I fire man
6.

Example 3

Example 4

Let us now look at the *functions* we can see in these four pieces of writing, and then attempt an interpretation of the way in which particular resources such as English and literacy enable voice for this pupils. What is it that we hear in these texts? In order to establish that, we again need to examine the details of these texts, starting with a transcript that brings out some of their formal features.

1. I want to be a teacher
   I want to hit the children who are rude in my class
   I will never be a bad teacher to the children in my class.
   I want a neat class.
   I want no bad smells in my class
   I want the children to wash every day
   I want to be a good teacher

2. I want to be a teacher so that I can teach the children like my teacher teach me.
   And I want to teach them what my teacher teach me
   And I would like to teach children that will listen to me every day.

3. 1 I soccer
   2. I pollce

```
3 I box
4 I player
¿ I fireman
6
```

```
4. enenenen
   neheneneen
   enenenen
   enerher
   enenken
```

The differences, as said, are enormous, but still we see remarkable similarities. In all four texts, we see that the pupils structure their writing as a list of coordinated, symmetrical utterances – rhymes, if we adopt the poetic perspective outlined earlier. This tendency to construct a list of ordered, symmetrical utterances is present even in 3 and 4 (even outspokenly so). The writing task, consequently, appears to trigger a move towards one of the most common and clear models for epistemic representation: the list (see also Fabian (1990) and Blommaert (2004)). Thus, we hear an epistemic voice, a particular articulation of knowledge, clearly regimented in a genre format: that of truncated, coordinated, symmetrical ordering.

We see more. If we turn to the two first examples and look more closely at the particular poetic organisation of both texts, we see some more informative distinctions.

1. **I want to be a teacher** ⇐
   I want to hit the children who are rude in my class
   I will never be a bad teacher to the children in my class. ⇐
   I want a neat class.
   I want no bad smells in my class
   I want the children to wash every day
   I want to be a good teacher ⇐

2. I want to be a teacher
> so that I can teach the children like *my teacher teach me.* ⇐
> And I want to teach them what *my teacher teach me* ⇐
> And I would like to teach children that will listen to me every
> day.

The poetic structure of both texts is very different. Text (1) is structured around one gradually developed motif: 'be a teacher' – 'never be a bad teacher' – 'be a good teacher'. The development of this motif proceeds through a series of qualifications of 'being a (good) teacher': to hit the bad pupils and to ensure that the class is neat. Text (2) elaborates the same motif of 'being a teacher', but does so emphatically by referring to the current teacher (*my* teacher) as a model.

While both texts are structured according to the epistemic model of a coordinated list, this epistemic mode includes affective and experiential voices too. In both texts, we see what being a teacher looks like from a pupil's perspective, and all sorts of implicit perspectives are articulated in the process. In text (1), the pupil focuses strongly on the disciplinary aspects of being a teacher, and we can assume that the remarks about a neat class, bad smells and unwashed pupils have their origins in the pupil's current negative experience of being in class: her class is probably not a good one for her. The same applies to the author of text (2): 'children that will listen to me every day' must refer to experiences of unruly classes where children do *not* listen to the teacher – hence the modal 'would like'. But in contrast to (1), text (2) articulates admiration for the current teacher. Recall that both pupils were in the same class and share the same teacher: the experience of the teacher's performance is different in both cases: (1) holds an implicitly negative image of her current class as being unruly and untidy; (2) admires the teacher and implicitly notes the fact that not all children listen to the teacher. Both pupils articulate a very different position vis-à-vis the same topic, and poetic analysis is able to bring that small difference out.

Both pupils achieve a delicate articulation of an epistemic, affective and experiential perspective, and they do so by means of literacy and English skills that show traces of 'peripheral normativity' (Blommaert *et al.* 2005): local criteria for what counts as 'good' English and 'good' writing. We are facing accent in writing, like in 'what my teacher teach me' and 'children that will listen to me' in text (2), and both pupils have some difficulty in using punctuation. Even our two very weak writers in (3) and (4) offer us glimpses – even if minimal ones – of the life worlds behind them. The author of (3) expresses a clear preference for manifestly masculine jobs: 'soccer' and 'player' probably belong together ('soccer player'), and if we add 'box' (boxer, fighter) we understand that our pupil is probably someone with sports ambitions. If we add 'pollce' (policeman) and 'fireman' to the list, we see that our pupil projects a very physical and masculine image of himself. As for the author of text (4), the remarkable thing is the fact that while two lines are identical ('enenenen'), the others are different. The author clearly tries to articulate something – what exactly is hard to guess, but something nevertheless. Minimally, he displays a basic understanding of genre, more specifically of the same genre as that used by the other pupils: an assignment such as this one needs to be organised as a list of coordinated utterances. For all four pupils, we see that writing has a basic function – to organise knowledge in a particular generically regimented way – and that for some it offers more – the articulation of delicate personal meanings rooted in experience, the capacity of voice.

The point to all this is to understand how English literacy resources penetrate a peripheral environment such as the township school near Cape Town. We see enormous differences in real capacity among the pupils, but we also see stability in basic genre realisation. Even our largely illiterate author of text (4) possesses that capacity; it doesn't buy him/her much, but it is there. So what is effectively globalised is one very old and very fundamental ideology of writing attached to one elementary function of writing: writing as an instrument for organising knowledge through particular genres such as lists, tables, enumerations. What is *not* effectively globalised is all the rest: the capacity to articulate complex personal meanings – voice – through English literacy is differentially distributed in this group even if it appears to be recognised by all four of our pupils, and the whole of the group performs a recognisably local 'township' form of English literacy. The end product is text produced by means of 'placed' resources: local English and local literacy skills.

Globalisation from the centre to the periphery is a process in which a lot is *not* carried over. More specifically, what is *not* carried over is the truly empowering potential of these resources, the way in which they should help people to make sense and be heard by means of them. It is this potential – lacking, unfortunately, for many in the periphery – that truly 'mainstreams' pupils.

Mainstreaming the immigrant

Let us now turn to the opposite direction, from the periphery to the centre. People with the kinds of 'placed' resources such as the ones discussed above travel, and like the Congolese woman whose text we examined earlier, find themselves in the large urban and literacy-saturated environments of the West. Their children go to school, and let us now consider what happens there. I will draw on work done in Dutch immersion classes in the Flemish part of Belgium in 2002–2003.[9] Newly immigrated children are defined as 'other-language newcomers' (*anderstalige nieuwkomers* in Dutch), and are brought into at least one year of Dutch immersion prior to being 'mainstreamed' in regular classes. Note that there is a very strong political-ideological undercurrent that supports this immersion tactic: in the context of migration, the Flemish Government increasingly emphasises the importance of Dutch as a prerequisite to 'integration' into the host society (see Blommaert and Verschueren (1998) for a general discussion). This phenomenon is another face of globalisation: while the flow from centre to periphery is characterised by international resources such as English, the flow from the periphery to the centre is captured in localism and regionalism. Immigrants in Belgium have to learn Dutch and French, not English; immigrants in Sweden need to learn Swedish, in Germany German, in Spain Spanish, and so on.

In earlier research (Blommaert *et al.* 2006b) we pointed out that immigrant children are being declared 'language-less' and illiterate when they enter such immersion classes. Their often intricate multilingual repertoires are not recognised and certainly not used as existing and valuable linguistic-communicative instruments, and pupils find themselves in an 'A-B-C' environment in which language and writing needs to be learned from scratch. Consequently, tremendous efforts are spent in acquiring highly specific formal writing skills such as the graphic shape of the 's' symbol below (the underlined form is the teacher's instruction):

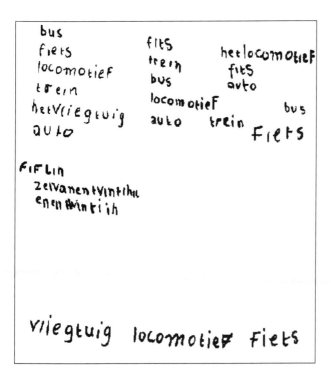

I want to focus on one particular piece of writing, produced by a 12-year-old boy from Bulgaria whom we shall call Sali (a pseudonym). The example below is a page from his copybook, in which he exercised his writing of dictated words.

Sali's writing shows signs of unfamiliarity with the writing conventions of Dutch. We see the unwarranted use of capitals ('Fiets', 'locomotieF') and difficulties in sequencing the graphic symbols into one uninterrupted string (as in 'vis' above): he writes separate symbols. Notwithstanding that, Sali's writing is largely correct, even when it comes to realising some of the more tricky peculiarities of the Dutch orthographic system such as the double symbols 'ui' and 'au'. The more interesting are the errors. Sali provides two versions of the Dutch word 'fiets' (bicycle): 'fiets' and 'fits'. And he also writes these two very peculiar forms:

Zeivanentvintihu
enentwintiih

Transliterated, these would read as 'zeivanentvintihi' and 'enentwintiih'. These are realisations of what in standard Dutch orthography would be 'zeventwintig' (twenty-seven) and 'eenentwintig' (twenty-one), respectively.

These forms are intensely interesting, because what Sali writes here is a very accurate graphic approximation of the *local Dutch accent of the teacher*. Sali's school was in Antwerp and his teacher was an Antwerp native. In the teacher's local accent, the distinction between long and short [i] sounds is unnoticeable, even if they are represented by two different graphemes, /i/ (short [i]) and /ie/ (long [iː]). So in the teacher's accent, the [i] in 'vis' and in 'fiets' would sound identical ([viːs] and [fiːts]), and this inaudible difference is reflected in Sali's use of both graphemes /i/ and /ie/. This is even more outspoken in the case of 'zeivanentvintihi': in the teacher's local accent, the word 'zeventwintig' ([zeːvənəntwɪntəɣ]) would be pronounced as [zævənəntwɪntəɣ], and this is precisely what Sali writes: he writes the Antwerp dialect accent that he hears from the teacher, using the conventional grapheme /ei/ for [æ]. Sali is freewheeling here. While most other forms he writes (e.g. 'locomotief') are the result of formal learning, he also experiments in his copybook, noting down new words he has heard – 'zevenentwintig' and 'eenentwintig' – or attempting to combine words with articles as in 'het locomotief' (which should be '*de* locomotief' – 'the locomotive'). In making these brave attempts, we see that Sali exploits what he has already learned in the way of orthographic logic, and that he simultaneously ventures into the many places where such logic is absent. In his 'enentwintiih', he writes the initial long [e:] as /e/: orthographically wrong, but understandable because long [e:] can also be written as /e/. In the same word, the [w] is correctly written as /w/, while in 'zeivanentvintihi' he wrote the same sound as /v/. Together with the final soft [ɣ] the [w] is notoriously hard to acquire for many non-native speakers of Dutch; the orthographic errors are thus understandable.

Sali produces voice here: the voice of an eager and enthusiastic learner who pushes the limits of his learning by experimenting with the resources he already has. Even if his writing skills suffer from basic imperfections – his use of capitals etc. – we see that it offers him a capacity to start reproducing and expanding the things he knows. His voice is, however, that of an immigrant: he records the local accent probably without an awareness that it is not a standard form of Dutch. Any Dutch is Dutch for those who do not know it (like any English is English for those who don't know it). The orthographic errors he produces, consequently, reveal his particular position vis-à-vis Dutch: that of a non-native learner in Antwerp, surrounded by local native accents and confronted with the compelling normativity of a standard orthography. His writing, in short, defines the immigrant learner.

The tension is easily sketched. Sali's writing reveals 'integration' in a real sociolinguistic environment. He picks up, perhaps also reproduces in speaking, the local accent of Dutch. He does that very well, and in that sense his writing skills are excellently developed. But his performance as a language learner will be judged on the basis not of the sociolinguistic reality in which he finds his place, but on the basis of a normative standard that only exists, for him, as a set of formal writing conventions (which can be seen from his alteration of /fits/ and /fiets/). Simply put: while his writing of 'zeivanentvintihi' is absolutely accurate as a replica of sociolinguistic reality, it is just an error when seen from the normative standard viewpoint. And so while from the first perspective Sali is fully integrated, he is not integrated from the second perspective. Unless we see his writing skills as skills for producing an experiential voice, we will be tempted to disqualify them as just 'bad writing'. Entering the mainstream, here, means being able to reproduce a strictly regimented set of skills, the function of which is just reflexive: to demonstrate that one can reproduce them.

Voice, choice and schools

What we have seen in these two sets of examples is how pupils construct voice under severe constraints on linguistic choice. In both examples, the pupils had to work in a medium that was not theirs, and they all clearly struggled with some of the basic skills they had to use. The effects of literacy and language, when perceived as normative and as vehicles for just a small set of stereotypical 'linguistic' functions, is that linguistic products are silenced and made invisible. The texts discussed in both examples are all very unremarkable and easy to dismiss as just trivia documenting a particular stage in a learning trajectory. I prefer to see them as little sites of struggle – a struggle to make sense and to make oneself understood under exacting and restraining conditions. Such conditions characterise much of what we understand by globalisation for many people who are part of globalisation processes: they are disabling rather than enabling, excluding rather than including, and repressing rather than liberating. Producing voice under such conditions is possible, but detecting it requires a tactic of examination that focuses on implicit patterns, on poetics rather than linguistics. It requires, in other words, a demanding and complex form of analysis – one, however, which I believe to be very necessary if we believe in equity and equality.

I am not the first to define schools as sites of struggle; indeed, this view is far from original and shared by generations of educational researchers. But we also need to understand schools as institutional environments in which the elementary processes of subjectivity – making yourself heard and understood by other people – can be and are problematic in an age of globalisation. People use all there is to use in making sense; they use explicit linguistic resources as well as implicit, sociocultural ones. If we solely focus on the explicit resources and deny the existence of the implicit ones, chances are that their voices are not identified, recognised and heard.

Conclusion: towards competence

The analytical point made in the previous sections was that, if we want to understand the role of language in the real lives of real people, we need to attend to function. And function should be established ethnographically, that is, on the basis of what counts as language and what language means for those who use it. We need to look carefully at the complex and infinitely sensitive ways in which people deploy often uncomfortable and clumsy linguistic tools in attempts to make sense.

That means that we need to use a much wider concept of competence – 'knowledge of a language' should not be restricted to the capacity to just perform linguistic functions. People appear to possess a much richer repertoire of competences, one that allows them to bypass the limitations of their purely linguistic competences, to add to them and to complement them. These are the competences we all enjoy and appreciate in everyday life: the competence to tell a good joke or to laugh when someone tells one, the competence to say kind words to someone in distress, to express our anger and anxiety whenever needed, to give others the feeling that they are cared about and listened to. It is the capacity to use language for fun, for pleasure and for effect – to impress, intimidate, or to mollify and give in. It is this complex of competences that makes people memorable: Nelson Mandela was a great orator, in spite of his heavy South African accent; Martin Luther King was an even greater one in spite of his Afro-American accent. And no one can remain unmoved when listening to speeches by Lumumba or Gandhi, even if both spoke with distinctly un-prestigious accents.

The tendency in the face of increasing super-diversity to withdraw into the safe fortresses of homogeneism in language and culture means, in our field, an increased emphasis on linguistic norms and rules and an increased standardisation of appraisal criteria for language performance in education. This is likely to reinforce the belief that meanings can only be produced in grammatically well-formed sentences, spoken in the right accent or written in the correct orthographic code. The stronger this emphasis – in itself a venerable educational target of all times – the more people will fail to match these criteria due to the factors that I hope to have clearly outlined here, and the more people will be excluded from those whose voices are being heard in society. In that sense, the belief that uniformity in rules, norms and procedures automatically generates a democratic environment is absurd. It will generate exactly the opposite in a globalised society: an increasingly small 'mainstream' surrounded by an increasingly big 'non-mainstream' population, the former fully enfranchised, the latter fully excluded. Democracy resides in doing justice to the really existing diversity, and this diversity requires ever more sophisticated analytic tactics to identify and recognise. My argument is: it requires structured and disciplined attention to the poetic forms that characterise communication, to what people actually do with language rather than to what we would like them to do.

Acknowledgement

This paper benefited seriously from substantive, critical and constructive comments by Gunther Kress, Ben Rampton and Mary Scott.

Notes

1. In December 2005, the Flemish government in Belgium decreed that people applying for social housing (a 'council flat' in the UK) would have to pass a basic Dutch language proficiency test in order to be eligible. In case of failure for that test, they would have to take a Dutch language course and pass a second test. Upon selection, they will get a two-year probation contract after which they would be assessed as to the timing of rent payments and the extent to which they cause 'nuisance' in their neighbourhoods. We see an implicit image of a 'good citizen' here, and the collocation of language and money in this image is of course intriguing.
2. The woman is left anonymous here. Such documents were sent to me by the Belgian police and courts for translation. I accepted their requests in return for permission to use the samples for research purposes. I never met any of the subjects, and apart from the kind of information given above, I have no further data on any of them.

3. This observation qualifies the often-heard optimism about literacy as liberating and emancipatory per se. See Blommaert (2004) for a discussion.

4. The term 'coloured', though clearly a remnant of Apartheid racial categories, is an official identity category in contemporary South Africa and it is also used as a self-qualifier. For a fuller discussion of this issue, see Maryns and Blommaert (2002), Blommaert *et al.* (2006a), and Verdoolaege (2007).

5. Maryns (2006) provides unparalleled detail on the interviewing practices in the Belgium asylum application interview. Aspects related to this analysis are also reported in Blommaert (2001) and Maryns and Blommaert (2001, 2005).

6. There is of course a whole story here, told much better by other people, about how the increasing emphasis on measurable ('objective') criteria fits into this utterly modernist and idealist (i.e. misconceived) idea of democracy, turning it into a technology of 'equal opportunities' which perpetuates existing inequalities. In our field, the European Profile for Language Teacher Education, the Programme for International Student Assessment (PISA) research programme, and the European language Levels could all illustrate the point. I have written about this in Dutch with reference to the development of policies in Belgium.

7. This research was developed in the context of the 'Dynamics of Building a Better Society' programme at the University of the Western Cape, funded by the Flemish Inter-University Council.

8. In a curious but not untypical twist, teachers rarely came in focus when issues of inequality in education were addressed. Teachers were seen as, in principle, all perfectly capable to fulfil the requirements of their jobs. The fact that Apartheid not only structured inequality among learners, but also among teachers, was and remains a rarely addressed topic.

9. I express my gratitude to the King Baudouin Foundation who funded this particular piece of research.

References

Appadurai, A. (1996) *Modernity at Large: Cultural dimensions of globalization.* Minneapolis: University of Minnesota Press.

Blommaert, J. (1998) 'English in a popular Swahili novel'. In J. Van der Auwera, F. Durieux and L. Lejeune (eds), *English as a Human Language. To honour Louis Goossens,* 22–31. Munich: LINCOM Europa.

— (2001) 'Investigating narrative inequality: African asylum seekers' stories in Belgium'. *Discourse & Society*, 12/4, 413–49.

— (2004) 'Writing as a problem: African grassroots writing, economies of literacy, and globalization'. *Language in Society*, 33, 643–71.

— (2005) *Discourse: A critical introduction*. Cambridge: Cambridge University Press.

Blommaert, J. and Verschueren, J. (1998) *Debating Diversity: Analysing the discourse of tolerance*. London: Routledge.

Blommaert, J., Huysmans, M., Muyllaert, N. and Dyers, C. (2005) 'Peripheral normativity: literacy and the production of locality in a South African township school'. *Linguistics and Education*, 16, 378–403.

Blommaert, J., Bock, M. and McCormick, K. (2006a) 'Narrative inequality in the TRC hearings: on the hearability of hidden transcripts'. *Journal of Language and Politics*, 5/1, 37–70.

Blommaert, J., Creve, L. and Willaert, E. (2006b) 'On being declared illiterate: language-ideological disqualification in Dutch classes for immigrants in Belgium'. *Language and Communication*, 26, 34–54.

Bourdieu, P. (1991) *Language and Symbolic Power*. Cambridge: Polity.

Bourdieu, P. and Passeron, J.-C. (1977) *La Réproduction: Eléments pour une théorie du système d'enseignement*. Paris: Minuit.

Castells, M. (1997) *The Power of Identity*. London: Blackwell.

Fabian, J. (1990) *History from Below: The 'Vocabulary of Elisabethville' by André Yav*. Amsterdam: John Benjamins.

Goffman, E. (1981) *Forms of Talk*. Philadelphia: University of Pennsylvania Press.

Hymes, D. (1981) *In Vain I Tried To Tell You: Essays in Native American ethnopoetics*. Philadelphia: University of Pennsylvania Press.

— (1996) *Ethnography, Linguistics, Narrative Inequality: Toward an understanding of voice*. London: Taylor & Francis.

— (2003) *Now I Know Only So Much: Essays in ethnopoetics*. Lincoln: University of Nebraska Press.

Maryns, K. (2006) *The Asylum Speaker: Language in the Belgian asylum procedure*. Manchester: St Jerome.

Maryns, K. and Blommaert, J. (2001) 'Stylistic and thematic shifting as narrative resources: assessing asylum seekers' repertoires'. *Multilingua*, 20/1, 61–84.

— (2002) 'Pretextuality and pretextual gaps: on re/defining linguistic inequality'. *Pragmatics*, 12/1, 11–30.

— (2005) 'Conducting dissonance: codeswitching and differential access to context in the Belgian asylum procedure'. In C. Mar-Molinero and P. Stevenson (eds), *Language Ideologies, Policies and Practices*, 177–190. London: Palgrave.

Verdoolaege, A. (2007) *The South African Truth and Reconciliation Commission: Deconstruction of a multilayered reconciliation discourse.* Amsterdam: John Benjamins.

Vertovec, S. (2006) 'The emergence of super-diversity in Britain' *Oxford University Centre on Migration, Policy and Society Working Paper 25.*

The Institute of Education Professorial Lecture series

Inaugural lectures by professors at the Institute of Education include the following titles. Please visit www.ioe.ac.uk/publications for more information about these and all our books and for ordering information.

Headship and beyond: the motivation and development of school leaders
Peter Earley

Learning to read
Morag Stuart

Whatever happened to the Dearing Report? UK higher education 1997–2007
David Watson

Writing in the academy: reputation, education and knowledge
Ken Hyland

Running ever faster down the wrong road: an alternative future for education and skills
Frank Coffield

Predictions, explanations and causal effects from longitudinal data
Ian Plewis

Bernstein and poetics revisited
Jan Blommaert

Only connect! Improving teaching and learning in schools
Mary James

The lifecycle of reform in education from the circumstances of birth to stages of decline: causes, ideologies and power relations
Miriam Ben-Peretz

The persistence of presentism and the struggle for lasting improvement
Andrew Hargreaves